Francis Frith's
Berkshire Churches

Photographic Memories

Francis Frith's
Berkshire Churches

David Parker

FRITH
Book Co

Published in the United Kingdom in 2000 by
Frith Book Company Ltd

British Library Cataloguing in Publication Data

Francis Frith's Berkshire Churches
David Parker
ISBN 1-85937-170-1

Frith Book Company Ltd
Frith's Barn, Teffont,
Salisbury, Wiltshire SP3 5QP
Tel: +44 (0) 1722 716 376
Email: info@frithbook.co.uk
www.frithbook.co.uk

Printed and bound in Great Britain

Acknowledgements

Wokingham Reference Library.
Mrs P Harfield, Archivist, Eton College Library.
The Buildings of England, Berkshire, by Nikolaus Pevsner. (Penguin Books, 1966).
The Buildings of England, Buckinghamshire, by Nikolaus Pevsner (Penguin Books, 1960/1994).
The Library of the Royal Military Academy, Sandhurst.
Maidenhead IT & Reference Library.
St Lawrence Hungerford Parish Church History (Tower Publications).
Murray's Buckinghamshire Architectural Guide (John Murray, 1948).
Victoria County History, Buckinghamshire. (St Catherine Press. Reprinted 1969).
Datchet Past by Janet Kennish (Phillimore, 1999).
St Mary's Church Maidenhead Calendar, Blotter and History 1930 (Bradmore, Birmingham).
Slough Reference Library.
Slough Express.
Slough Observer.

Much of the editorial in this book was compiled from material from the above-named sources and publications.

Contents

Front Cover: Sonning, St Andrew's Church 1890 27160

Francis Frith: *Victorian Pioneer*

FRANCIS FRITH, Victorian founder of the world-famous photographic archive, was a complex and multitudinous man. A devout Quaker and a highly successful Victorian businessman, he was both philosophic by nature and pioneering in outlook.

By 1855 Francis Frith had already established a wholesale grocery business in Liverpool, and sold it for the astonishing sum of £200,000, which is the equivalent today of over £15,000,000. Now a multi-millionaire, he was able to indulge his passion for travel. As a child he had pored over travel books written by early explorers, and his fancy and imagination had been stirred by family holidays to the sublime mountain regions of Wales and Scotland. 'What a land of spirit-stirring and enriching scenes and places!' he had written. He was to return to these scenes of grandeur in later years to 'recapture the thousands of vivid and tender memories', but with a different purpose. Now in his thirties, and captivated by the new science of photography, Frith set out on a series of pioneering journeys to the Nile regions that occupied him from 1856 until 1860.

Intrigue and Adventure

He took with him on his travels a specially-designed wicker carriage that acted as both dark-room and sleeping chamber. These far-flung journeys were packed with intrigue and adventure. In his life story, written when he was sixty-three, Frith tells of being held captive by bandits, and of fighting 'an awful midnight battle to the very point of surrender with a deadly pack of hungry, wild dogs'. Sporting flowing Arab costume, Frith arrived at Akaba by camel seventy years before Lawrence, where he encountered 'desert princes and rival sheikhs, blazing with jewel-hilted swords'.

During these extraordinary adventures he was assiduously exploring the desert regions bordering the Nile and patiently recording the antiquities and peoples with his camera. He was the first photographer to venture beyond the sixth cataract. Africa was still the mysterious 'Dark Continent', and Stanley and Livingstone's historic meeting was a decade into the future. The conditions for picture taking confound belief. He laboured for hours in his wicker dark-room in the sweltering heat of the desert, while the volatile chemicals fizzed dangerously in their trays. Often he was forced to work in remote tombs and caves where conditions were cooler. Back in London he exhibited his photographs and was 'rapturously cheered' by members of the Royal Society. His reputation as a photographer was made overnight. An eminent modern historian has likened their impact on the population of the time to that on our own generation of the first photographs taken on the surface of the moon.

Venture of a Life-Time

Characteristically, Frith quickly spotted the opportunity to create a new business as a specialist publisher of photographs. He lived in an era of immense and sometimes violent change. For the poor in the early part of Victoria's reign work was a drudge and the hours long, and people had precious little free time to enjoy themselves. Most had no transport other than a cart or gig at their disposal, and had not travelled far beyond the

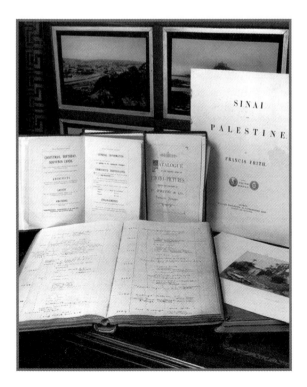

boundaries of their own town or village. However, by the 1870s, the railways had threaded their way across the country, and Bank Holidays and half-day Saturdays had been made obligatory by Act of Parliament. All of a sudden the ordinary working man and his family were able to enjoy days out and see a little more of the world.

With characteristic business acumen, Francis Frith foresaw that these new tourists would enjoy having souvenirs to commemorate their days out. In 1860 he married Mary Ann Rosling and set out with the intention of photographing every city, town and village in Britain. For the next thirty years he travelled the country by train and by pony and trap, producing fine photographs of seaside resorts and beauty spots that were keenly bought by millions of Victorians. These prints were painstakingly pasted into family albums and pored over during the dark nights of winter, rekindling precious memories of summer excursions.

The Rise of Frith & Co

Frith's studio was soon supplying retail shops all over the country. To meet the demand he gathered about him a small team of photographers, and published the work of independent artist-photographers of the calibre of Roger Fenton and Francis Bedford. In order to gain some understanding of the scale of Frith's business one only has to look at the catalogue issued by Frith & Co in 1886: it runs to some 670 pages, listing not only many thousands of views of the British Isles but also many photographs of most European countries, and China, Japan, the USA and

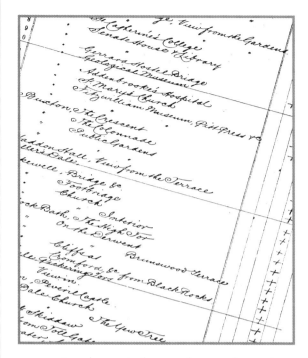

Canada – note the sample page shown above from the hand-written *Frith & Co* ledgers detailing pictures taken. By 1890 Frith had created the greatest specialist photographic publishing company in the world, with over 2,000 outlets – more than the combined number that Boots and WH Smith have today! The picture on the right shows the *Frith & Co* display board at Ingleton in the Yorkshire Dales. Beautifully constructed with mahogany frame and gilt inserts, it could display up to a dozen local scenes.

Postcard Bonanza

The ever-popular holiday postcard we know today took many years to develop. In 1870 the Post Office issued the first plain cards, with a pre-printed stamp on one face. In 1894 they allowed other publishers' cards to be sent through the mail with an attached adhesive halfpenny stamp. Demand grew rapidly, and in 1895 a new size of postcard was permitted called the court card, but there was little room for illustration. In 1899, a year after Frith's death, a new card measuring 5.5 x 3.5 inches became the standard format, but it was not until 1902 that the divided back came into being, with address and message on one face and a full-size illustration on the other. *Frith & Co* were in the vanguard of postcard development, and Frith's sons Eustace and Cyril continued their father's monumental task, expanding the number of views offered to the public and recording more and more places in Britain, as the coasts and country-side were opened up to mass travel.

Francis Frith died in 1898 at his villa in Cannes, his great project still growing. The archive he created continued in business for another seventy years. By 1970 it contained over a third of a million pictures of 7,000 cities, towns and villages. The massive photographic record Frith has left to us stands as a living monument to a special and very remarkable man.

Frith's Archive: *A Unique Legacy*

FRANCIS FRITH'S legacy to us today is of immense significance and value, for the magnificent archive of evocative photographs he created provides a unique record of change in 7,000 cities, towns and villages throughout Britain over a century and more. Frith and his fellow studio photographers revisited locations many times down the years to update their views, compiling for us an enthralling and colourful pageant of British life and character.

We tend to think of Frith's sepia views of Britain as nostalgic, for most of us use them to conjure up memories of places in our own lives with which we have family associations. It often makes us forget that to Francis Frith they were records of daily life as it was actually being lived in the cities, towns and villages of his day. The Victorian age was one of great and often bewildering change for ordinary people, and though

the pictures evoke an impression of slower times, life was as busy and hectic as it is today.

We are fortunate that Frith was a photographer of the people, dedicated to recording the minutiae of everyday life. For it is this sheer wealth of visual data, the painstaking chronicle of changes in dress, transport, street layouts, buildings, housing, engineering and landscape that captivates us so much today. His remarkable images offer us a powerful link with the past and with the lives of our ancestors.

Today's Technology

Computers have now made it possible for Frith's many thousands of images to be accessed almost instantly. In the Frith archive today, each photograph is carefully 'digitised' then stored on a CD Rom. Frith archivists can locate a single photograph amongst thousands within seconds. Views can be catalogued and sorted under a variety of categories of place and content to the immediate benefit of researchers.

Inexpensive reference prints can be created for them at the touch of a mouse button, and a wide range of books and other printed materials assembled and published for a wider, more general readership - in the next twelve months over a hundred Frith local history titles will be published! The day-to-day workings of the archive are very different from how they were in Francis Frith's time: imagine the herculean task of sorting through eleven tons of glass negatives as Frith had to do to locate a particular

See Frith at www. frithbook.co.uk

sequence of pictures! Yet the archive still prides itself on maintaining the same high standards of excellence laid down by Francis Frith, including the painstaking cataloguing and indexing of every view.

It is curious to reflect on how the internet now allows researchers in America and elsewhere greater instant access to the archive than Frith himself ever enjoyed. Many thousands of individual views can be called up on screen within seconds on one of the Frith internet sites, enabling people living continents away to revisit the streets of their ancestral home town, or view places in Britain where they have enjoyed holidays. Many overseas researchers welcome the chance to view special theme selections, such as transport, sports, costume and ancient monuments.

We are certain that Francis Frith would have heartily approved of these modern developments in imaging techniques, for he himself was always working at the very limits of Victorian photographic technology.

The Value of the Archive Today

Because of the benefits brought by the computer, Frith's images are increasingly studied by social historians, by researchers into genealogy and ancestory, by architects, town planners, and by teachers and schoolchildren involved in local history projects.

In addition, the archive offers every one of us an opportunity to examine the places where we and our families have lived and worked down the years. Highly successful in Frith's own era, the archive is now, a century and more on, entering a new phase of popularity.

The Past in Tune with the Future

Historians consider the Francis Frith Collection to be of prime national importance. It is the only archive of its kind remaining in private ownership and has been valued at a million pounds. However, this figure is now rapidly increasing as digital technology enables more and more people around the world to enjoy its benefits.

Francis Frith's archive is now housed in an historic timber barn in the beautiful village of Teffont in Wiltshire. Its founder would not recognize the archive office as it is today. In place of the many thousands of dusty boxes containing glass plate negatives and an all-pervading odour of photographic chemicals, there are now ranks of computer screens. He would be amazed to watch his images travelling round the world at unimaginable speeds through network and internet lines.

The archive's future is both bright and exciting. Francis Frith, with his unshakeable belief in making photographs available to the greatest number of people, would undoubtedly approve of what is being done today with his lifetime's work. His photographs, depicting our shared past, are now bringing pleasure and enlightenment to millions around the world a century and more after his death.

Berkshire Churches

an introduction

What is a church?
Our honest sexton tells,
'Tis a tall building,
With a tower and bells.
(George Crabbe; 1754-1832)

The Royal County

BERKSHIRE IS NOW made up of unitary authorities without a county council administration. Before 1974, it was relatively small, long and narrow, tucked between Oxford and Buckingham to the north, and Surrey and Hampshire in the south. The name means 'wooded hill district'. Its main towns are Reading in the centre, which has eight churches and an abbey ruins, and

Hungerford to the far west. Windsor, with its famous castle, St George's Chapel and eight churches is on the eastern extreme, on the outskirts of London. Slough, Newbury, Wokingham, Bracknell and Maidenhead are other major centres.

Known as the Royal County of Berkshire, it was divided into unitary authorities under local government reorganisation in the 1990s.

Although Windsor Castle, the famous landmark and home of the monarchy, dominates, Berkshire is unlike many other old-established counties because it has no large urban development other than the unitary authority of Slough; nor does it boast a cathedral. The changes to the county boundary have had a marked effect on the total history of the area because, for instance, some of the former trading towns like Wantage found themselves in neighbouring counties, particularly Oxfordshire, after the re-shuffle; but within its boundaries, new Berkshire still retains the world-famous public school Eton, the military academy at Sandhurst, and a variety of renowned successful racing stables at Lambourn. The major motorway M4 cuts almost through the middle of the old county.

In his book 'Berkshire' - part of the 'Buildings of England' series published by Penguin Books - Nikolaus Pevsner describes the county as 'half home counties and half west country', pointing out that its downs link into Wiltshire. He claims that the county is 'a bonanza of High Anglo-Catholic communities'. The west of Berkshire marks the northern limits of the brilliant Wessex Culture which had so much influence on the middle years of the 20th century. Without a source of local stone, Portland and Bath stone were the most commonly-used building materials for churches at this time. The predominantly chalk soil threw up a lot of flints which were also put to good use, with a natural dark brown cement known as puddlestone used for binding the flints and pebbles and small pieces of sandstone during construction work.

Flint tools - mainly axe heads dating from the Old Stone Age - have been found in gravel deposits. This is most evident in the group of churches around Wokingham, such as Binfield, Warfield and Winkfield. The Palaeolithic Age settlements were established mainly along river valleys, and isolated boulders of tough sandstone - known as Berkshire sarsens - can be found all over the county, often used as corner-stones, stepping stones, gate posts and walls. Some houses were built with sarsens and can be found at Lambourn, Ashbury and Idstone, and it was a material used very extensively in Windsor Castle.

Some churches have been 'wrecked by 19th-century restoration work' in the east of the county, according to Pevsner, which is mostly a dormitory of London. In the west of the county, however, he believes some 'gems' remain; but there is nothing pre-Conquest, and the Norman period presents a bleak picture; most numerous are Gothic examples. It is also apparent that Berkshire did not accept the Italian Renaissance too readily or enthusiastically.

Yet, suffice it to say, all the Berkshire churches, rural and urban, have individual merit and are worthy of a visit. Some have

more than the usual awe-inspiring ambience; and some have their own strange tale attached. For instance, at Yattendon there are reports that the Old Rectory was once haunted by the most charming ghost in England. Dressed in black watered silk, she was a party lover and would lead rectors' wives to undiscovered hens' nests when there were no eggs in the house. She was always in a hurry and was as mysterious as she was useful. In life, she was said to be the unmarried sister of an 18th-century rector. Exorcism has apparently temporarily banished this soul.

Church architecture from the Saxons to George IV fall into six distinct patterns. Before 1066, the Saxons built square functional places of worship in wood and stone. Most of the wooden churches have disappeared, but stone buildings survive as parts of cathedrals, monasteries and large churches. In the Norman period, between 1066 and 1180, large edifices were typified by thick walls and flat buttresses, with round arches, vigorous ornament and a simple plan. In many existing parish churches the earliest part of the structure dates from this period. Pointed arches were introduced in the Early English period from 1160 to 1310. The ground plan is enlarged to include an aisle and a porch to the south door. Tall narrow windows have little or no tracery. From 1300 to 1380, the Decorated period can be identified by the elaborate geometrical window tracery and abundant ornamental carving. In Salisbury Cathedral the parapet walls hide the base of the spire. Buttresses and columns take most of the weight of designs in the Perpendicular period from 1350 to 1550. Walls were free to accommodate large windows, giving a sense of light and space. Classic ornament and galleries with flat ceilings marked the break with Gothic when the Renaissance period took over in 1550, lasting until 1840.

Berkshire has little to offer of Elizabethan and Jacobean architecture and art, but it has sufficient history to build up a sequence of transition from Late Norman to mature Early English, through the development of the square abacus of round piers becoming octagonal and then round; we can also see the round arches becoming pointed, and the heavily roll-moulded arch replaced by the slightly then fully chamfered or double-chamfered arch. In Berkshire, the square abacus still appears with waterleaf capitals of around 1170-80. At St Lawrence church, Reading, stiff leaf of 1196 is used. After 1250, plate tracery, then bar tracery, and finally intersecting and Y tracery precedes the pointed-trefoil lights, and their grouping into three stepped ones under an arch was liked in Berkshire.

Churches are not just buildings, of course, because each houses a wealth of individual characteristics in their pulpits, towers, windows (stained glass and plain), monuments and furniture. At Windsor, St George's Chapel,

which was started in 1475 by Edward IV, took 50 years to complete, by which time Henry VIII was king. The chapel was enlarged to accommodate members of the Order of the Garter created by Edward III in 1348, and it replaced Henry III's chapel further east. It has been a Royal burial place since the time of Henry VII, who died in 1509, but the remains of earlier monarchs were transferred here from the earlier chapels. It has glorious fan vaulting with much detail to admire, but the chapel has had so much restoration, mainly in the past 100 years, that details can only rarely be accepted as the original carvers' work. According to Mr Maurice Bond, Wren removed the original King's Beasts and repaired the roof and vault after 1682. Emlyn was responsible for repairing stonework and adding screen, stalls and staircase to the Royal Pew. Then in 1841-45, Blore reconstructed the west window; he was followed by Scott, who reconstructed the east end of the chancel in 1863. From 1866 to 1872, he also put in a new west approach. From 1878 to 1886, Pearson included new buttresses, parapets, and gargoyles in his restoration work. As recently as 1920 to 1930, Brakspear undertook a complete restoration and inserted new King's Beasts.

The Great Fire of 1992 was contained from spreading to the chapel, so today, the 700 Garter stall plates, the curious iron almsbox (marked with a repeated h -a sign that it was

probably for offerings to the cult of Henry VI near his tomb, over which his helmet hangs) and 96 misericords by William Berkeley and others of 1478-85 can be admired. An unusual brass of about 1630 features a child in a cradle, and a painting of the Last Supper by Benjamin West hangs in the vestry. A fine piece of 15th-century English smithy work by Cornish blacksmith John Tresilian can be found as an iron screen to Edward IV's chantry. Chantries themselves should be listed as church monuments because of their importance in history.

Many more treasures abound in St George's chapel, but the luxury for the historians and visitors to this example of a place of worship must not be allowed to overshadow the offerings of the other Windsor churches, or, indeed, of the many other delightful churches in the towns and villages of Berkshire. The wealth of numerous furnishings and monuments in the county date back to the late 13th century; among them, Aldworth has a series of eight monuments, six of which are under ornate but drastically restored canopies. One of these ladies is in the arrangement of the drapery in the cathedral tradition of the 13th century, and one of the men is cross-legged as is universally conventional in England, although absent on the continent; but his whole body writhes and twists.

At Childrey, a cross-legged knight in a

recess with ballflower decoration characterises this early 14th-century motif. In Hampstead Norris church, a mysterious relief more than 2ft high is of a man on horseback, also late 13th-century, and very skilfully done; but what did it belong to? Didcot has a late 13th-century mitred abbot of Purbeck marble, and Long Wittenham posses an amazing late 13th-century miniature stone effigy built into a piscina. Major examples of tomb monuments include recumbent figures made of alabaster in Bisham, Appleton, Speen, Tilehurst, Arborfield, and also at Radley, where the effigy by Nicholas Stone is of some interest. Frontal demi-figures were usual for scholars and divines. Small brass plates with upright or kneeling figures appear around the county, often framed in stone, perhaps with guilloche or an egg-and-dart motif. The finest Jacobean monument is that of Margaret Hoy at Bisham dated 1605, which is an obelisk carried by four swans with a heart on top.

Paintings of note include the beautiful early 14th-century Annunciation at Enborne, and some figures at Kingston Lisle and Aldermaston of the same period. The best example of late Mediaeval ceiling painting is perhaps in one of the chancel chapels at Abingdon, now in Oxfordshire.

Stained glass examples span most of the six major architectural periods of church building styles; the east window in the south chapel at North Moreton is typical of the styles of around 1300-1310. Church furnishings follow the national rule that there was very little done in the late 16th century; some examples are undated and may be Elizabethan, as in the case of the exceptionally fine pulpit with Floris motifs at Aldworth.

As part of a European history of art and architecture, England would contribute to the 50 years between 1615 and 1665 the work of Inigo Jones, Pratt, Webb, May and others until Wren, which indicates the spread of Palladian styles. Of great interest must be the fact that churches built after 1600 are few; Shrivenham, now in Oxfordshire, is the major example, dated at around 1638.

Churchyard gateways which are noteworthy include the pair at Newbury parish church, possibly by Fuller White in 1770 or so, which hint at a Gothic revival within the Picturesque period. In the early 1800s, typical churches took on Gothic influences, but their composition and internal space were still wedded to classical Georgian ideals. Known as Commissioners' Churches, examples include Windsor parish church of 1820-22, Hungerford of 1816, Sunninghill of 1826-27, Holy Trinity, Windsor, after 1837 and Bear Wood of 1846.

Victorian church buildings designed by those who came after Pugin appear in Bradfield, where Scott's parish church is one of the oldest of the type, dated 1847-48, and is a first class example of the change. Another

Pugin church for comparison is St James, Reading, 1837-40, which also shows Norman influences. Original church furnishings of the Victorian era often pass unnoticed: round stone pulpits, low iron screens, carved fonts - these are too little appreciated, according to some commentators, who also mention the weakness of Victorian sculpture, particularly the reredoses. In stained glass colouring and composition, the two most noted names are Morris and Kempe, and the county is rich in Victorian stained glass by Hardman, Wailes, Clayton and Bell and others.

In summary, the best of Berkshire churches cannot be quantified, but the best pulpit is probably the 1607 version at Newbury; the best 16th-century tower is at Warfield; and the best monument is the reclining alabaster effigies of Sir Philip and Sir Thomas Hoby (1558 and 1566 respectively) at Bisham, where Margaret Hoby is dignified by an obelisk carried by four swans with a heart on top, dated 1605. At Binfield there is an elaborate hourglass which is a central stem supporting alternating branches, some with oak leaves and acorns or grapes, shields, and the arms of the Farriers Company of London. This is a fine example with a lion and a pelican and a wolf worked in, showing off the blacksmith's art to the full and probably dates back to 1629.

Sometimes a single memory is conjured up by something seen or heard in a church which comes to mind when mentioned or remembered. It might be woodwork, ironwork, paintings, windows, architecture, art, decoration, style, tombs and other monuments, and even pews, pulpits and lecterns. Neglect through lack of money - and restoration - have made their mark on some edifices. Many churches have fallen into disrepair, and some are now unused for worship. Church architecture, design and materials are often influenced by, or are an influence on the types of buildings erected in their locality. Some may say that the architects of churches and other ecclesiastical foundations, such as church dwellings, monasteries, abbeys and priories, had too much influence on designs of mansions, public buildings and even private houses during their respective periods of artistic power, innovation and construction.

Development in old Berkshire, the wooded hill district tucked between London and the west country, could well have been influenced through the ages by its close proximity to London and the city's growth as an important capital centre of the commercial world and heart of a modern empire. As the Royal county, it has been overshadowed by Windsor Castle at one end and its vast rural expanses at the opposite end.

Suffice it to say, that as an immediate long-lasting reminder and living glimpse of history, churches have a very large part to play in our lives; and Berkshire's churches are no exception to this claim.

ASCOT, ALL SOULS CHURCH 1901 46860

Attributed to Pearson and built in the Early English style, this large, red-brick church was built in 1896-7, so it was relatively new in Francis Frith's photograph. The square crossing tower has an unexpected pyramidal roof, possibly in place of an intended spire. The Baptistry extends and projects to the south at the west end like a porch, and has two rounded angle buttresses with solid pinnacles. The main north porch has a small south porch attached to the angle between nave and transept. The brick interior, with four-bay arcades, is not emphatic; there is a rib-vaulted crossing and sexpartite rib-vaults in the chancel and the lower south chapel. The baptistry is also rib-vaulted; it is octagonal, with three open sides projecting into the south aisle. Its windows are a high three-light in the west and a broader five-light in the east.

◆

ASCOT, SOUTH ASCOT CHURCH 1901 46871

This modest building of red brick is attributed to T H Rushforth and was built in about 1864. The windows are 13th century and show a variety of designs in two-bay arcades. The Jesse stained glass window on the east is by Kempe, 1907, and the rose window above is by Hardman. The painting of chancel and aisles is by Heaton, Butler and Bayne around 1874 and 1883.

ASCOT, CHURCH 1903 50696

Inside All Saints, the feeling is of space and width, which emphasises the modesty of the design but allows the visitor to notice the many small fine touches which add atmosphere and elegance.

ASCOT, ST FRANCIS'S ROMAN CATHOLIC CHURCH 1901 46873

This church was built around 1889 by A J Scoles in red brick; it has an apse but no tower. It has strong aisles, octagonal piers, some lancet windows and other windows with plate tracery.

BINFIELD, ALL SAINTS CHURCH 1901 46905

From the Perpendicular period, with a west tower of a dark brown conglomerate, All Saints is much acclaimed for its setting. The prominent stair-turret has an ornate ogee top and is Victorian. The south aisle is built of conglomerate too. The north aisle is of 1848 and the east end is mostly of 1859; the rest is Perpendicular, except a south aisle window, which with its cusped Y-tracery must be from the 1300s. The south doorway has fleurons in one moulding. The Perpendicular four-bay arcades of octagonal piers have moulded arches. However, the south chapel arcade may be somewhat earlier.

BINFIELD, ALL SAINTS CHURCH c1955 B97010

An angel has appeared from a former house in the south chapel; the pulpit is dated 1628, and has blank arches and arabesque decoration; the back panel upper half has caryatids and the tester has strapwork cresting. An hourglass on an elaborate iron stand carries the arms of the Farriers' Company, London, and is a unique expression of the blacksmith's art of the time - 17th century - with leaves and grapes, a lion, a pelican and a wolf, attributed to Hurst. Victorian iron screens are on the west, north and south of the chancel. The 15th-century stained glass shows whole figures in the south-east window; the south aisle window, in violent colours, is by O'Connor and dates from 1863. The church monuments include a 9-inch bust, and inscriptions of the mid 16th century; on the reverse part of a figure of a bishop or abbot is a tablet with relief profile in a circular wreath and another tablet with flag and sabre and various brasswork.

BISHAM, ALL SAINTS CHURCH AND THE ABBEY 1890 23699

Bisham's two principal buildings, the church and the abbey, are highlighted by a backdrop of wooded hillsides. In the riverscape on which they both sit, they are not visually connected. The Norman church's west tower is very close to the Thames, and is easily recognised by its single-chamfered bell-openings. The tower arch is round, with one respond with a multi-scalloped capital and the other with waterleaf, dating the tower to around 1170-80. Much of the church seems to have had restoration work, except the Hoby Chapel, which has no windows and a chalk wall of the late 16th century. In the north chapel, the reredos includes four late Gothic painted saints, probably East Anglian. The Royal Arms of George II are painted with a guilloche frame, and the stained glass in the east window of the old Chapel has interesting heraldic glass from 1609.

BISHAM, ALL SAINTS, THE LYCHGATE 1890 23701

This early photograph depicts the image of village life at the end of the 19th century, showing a contrast of wooden fencing materials, one modern, the other very ancient like the church. The gate-house is simply designed, using wood and tiles. Bisham Abbey was only an abbey for three years: it was first a preceptory of the Templars, then in 1337 an Augustinian priory, then a Benedictine abbey in 1537, which was dissolved in 1540. The estate was granted to Sir Philip Hoby in 1553, and he began to build almost at once. After he died in 1558, his half brother continued until his death in 1566. Commentators say that the appearance of the buildings are complex and not easily understood. For instance, the south front has a 13th-century porch with a fine outer and an equally fine inner doorway and a quadripartite rib-vault. The doorways have colonnettes and extremely delicately-moulded arches. The doors are carried on ironwork. The part of the front east of the porch is also Hoby work, with chalk below stepped brick gables in which there are windows with mullion and transom crosses and their pediments. The Templars Hall seems to indicate that this Templars' house was not at all laid out like a monastery, but more like a manor house. The Augustinians supplied the cloisters, but only one range survived. Nearby barns have been converted into dwellings, and a circular dovecote was part of this setting.

BISHAM, INSIDE ALL SAINTS 1890 23703

The Hobys dominate the imposing monuments in the south chapel. The earliest is that of Sir Philip in 1558 and Sir Thomas of 1566. It is of alabaster, and is a tomb chest with the two bearded half brothers relaxed in semi-recumbent poses. Behind is a shallow arch in which is a long poem, worth reading in full. Sir Thomas's widow Elizabeth married Lord Russell, who died in 1583; she died in 1609. She is seen kneeling in widow's weeds under a canopy with columns. Behind her is a group of children and other figures outside the columns. This is also in alabaster, and contained in iron railings. Margaret, wife of Sir Edward who died in 1605, is also remembered among these fine, delicately and intricately-worked alabaster monuments. Other monuments in the church include a Purbeck tomb in the north chapel; this is a short tomb chest and canopy of three hanging arches on colonnettes with lozenge patterns. There is a pretty vault inside. It probably dates from the early 16th century, with the name Thomas Crekett of 1517. A brass in the nave west wall, a 16in figure relating to George Kenneth Vansittart who died in 1904 aged 14, shows a kneeling Eton schoolboy by Morris Harding under a Gothic canopy.

CAVERSHAM, ST PETER'S CHURCH 1904 52031
This fine river view of St Peter's Church, Caversham, now part of Reading, could almost be a water colour.

CAVERSHAM, ST PETER'S CHURCH 1913 65923
One can see immediately the Norman influence of the church; it lies
above the site of Caversham Court, now a public garden by the Thames.

CAVERSHAM, ST PETER'S CHURCH 1908 59975

In this incredible photograph, the orderliness of the church setting and burial ground become three-dimensional. The church's Norman doorway to the south is not shown, but it is mainly of shafts with zigzag up the jambs and in the arch, partly at right angles to the wall. Finer Norman points include a reset window in the west wall of the north vestry. The north wall is actually of the Perpendicular period; the south aisle is an addition of 1878, at which time the tower was rebuilt. Inside, low arcades with round piers have been maintained, and the north chapel is a good example of Perpendicular. Panelled arches are on a pier with carved angel-busts and a Windsor motif. The chapel has a north window which was added a little later than the other north windows. In 1924-25, the chancel was lengthened by Sir Norman Comper. Many fine features include a Norman font of Purbeck marble, which has a round basin but raised spurs with concave outlines at the angles; a brass chandelier dated 1743; a former wind vane of 1663, now on a staff; and a silver-gilt Elizabethan Revival flagon and two patens inscribed 1753.

◆

CHIEVELEY, THE MANOR AND ST MARY'S CHURCH C1955 C443025

This splendid setting shows off St Mary's alongside Chieveley Manor
House, which is of red brick with a hipped roof. The church is
unbuttressed, with a west tower and Perpendicular bell-stage and a
very fine chancel all dating back to the 13th century. The east wall
has three lancets with continuous roll mouldings outside and again
inside, where the shafts have stiff-leaf capitals. In the roof is one tie-
beam on arched braces with traceried spandrels, probably also
supporting the lenten veil. Side walls have lancets. The nave is
probably about 1873 by J W Hugall, and the font is octagonal,
Perpendicular with quatrefoils. Blank arches and arabesques mark
the Jacobean pulpit. One monument of note is the small tomb of
Mrs Fincher, 1688, with its square brass plate in a stone surround of
leathery or doughy forms of earlier years' influence, say of the 1650s.

COOKHAM, HOLY TRINITY CHURCH 1890 23669

The setting may have changed dramatically over the years, but Holy Trinity, not far from the Thames, remains as a flint-built church with some stone and a low broad tower to the west end. Nave and aisles and chancel chapels may be from different eras, but the nave is Norman, as one window indicates. In the early 13th century, the short north aisle and north chapel were built with lancet windows and a wide, low arch with nailhead ornaments to the chancel. Actually, the Victorian County History says the Norman-looking jambs of a two-bay arcade are 'modern'. One doorway is late 13th-century and blocked. At about the same time the south aisle and south arcade were built and the north arcade was remodelled. The south chapel is 14th-century, and it has two tomb recesses. An oddly-placed second doorway in the south aisle is an anomaly. The late Perpendicular west tower has a higher stair turret, and there are signs of 18th-century repairs in brick, with tie beams in the roof and kingposts to the north chapel.

COOKHAM, HOLY TRINITY CHURCH C1955 C157016

The east window stained glass is from about 1840. Among the monuments on the north side of the chancel is a Purbeck marble tomb with canopy and three hanging arches on twisted columns marked by an 18in brass on the short tomb chest. Here lies Robert Peake, who died in 1517, and his wife. Members of the Babham family are remembered in brasses, but the interesting memorial is that to Sir Isaac Pocock, who drowned in the Thames in 1810. By Flaxman, in white relief, his reclining body lies in a boat held by his niece with an oarsman in shallow relief behind.

COOKHAM DEAN, CHURCH OF ST JOHN BAPTIST 1950 C353003

Another picturesque but humble flint church built in about 1844 by Benjamin Ferrey, St John Baptist's church has a nave, chancel, low south aisle and bellcote in early 14th-century style. The interior is pure white. In the chancel is an example of good stained glass of about 1860, described as consciously primitive but with odd tensions in the faces, almost like Toorop, perhaps influenced by Moxon's Tennyson. A later window of 1893 in the north wall is by Kempe, and is primarily of dark brown and dark red.

CROWTHORNE, CHURCH OF ST JOHN BAPTIST 1914 66792

This photograph shows that St John Baptist's lychgate is a very fine strong statement at the entrance to a strong 19th-century brick-built church.

CROWTHORNE, CHURCH OF ST JOHN BAPTIST 1914 66794

Blomfield designed and built this church in 1873; the chancel was added in 1888-89. The materials he used were red bricks with black brick bands. The eye-catching steep bellcote over the nave on the east gable sets this church apart from most. The aisles are cross-gabled with geometrical tracery; a low apsed west baptistry is offset from the wide interior - it is also red and black brick with unmoulded brick arches. Stained glass in the east and south east windows is dated 1894 and 1889 respectively.

DATCHET, ST MARY'S CHURCH 1905

St Mary's Church was rebuilt between 1858 and
1860 from a design by Raphael Brandon. It is an
odd structure 'with an ornate octagonal north-east
tower on an odd superstructure and continued in
the oddest cross-gabled north transept and outer
north aisle', according to Nikolaus Pevsner in his
book on Buckinghamshire (Penguin: Buildings
of England series, 1960).

DATCHET, ST MARY'S CHURCH C1955

The village of Datchet, which has an intricate and
absorbing history, is known as the Royal Village, and
was in Buckinghamshire before the 1970s county
boundary changes. St Mary's has fine examples of
Victorian stained glass of 1860-65,
mostly by O'Connor.

DATCHET, ST MARY'S CHURCH 1905 53199

DATCHET, ST MARY'S CHURCH C1955 D9060

DATCHET, ST MARY'S CHURCH C1955 D9061

Three cartouches with individual busts on top commemorate Mary
Delaune (nee Wheeler), 1626, Hanbury Wheeler, 1633 and John
Wheeler 1636. This family's unhappy fortunes and failure to keep
the name alive is detailed in a book by Janet Kennish: 'Datchet
Past' (Phillimore, 1999). Sir William Wheeler is described as Lord
of Datchet Manor. In 1631, Charles I sold the Manor to Sir
Charles Harbord, surveyor to the king, who sold it on to Sir
William, who left the Manor to his young son William in 1649. It is
regrettable that he died before maturity. His seven sisters laid claim
to the Manor; the eldest, Ann Pitcairne, alias Wheeler, won and her
son sold it on in 1680 to Bud Wase.

◆

EARLEY, READING, ST PETER'S CHURCH 1910 62210A

St Peter's is Early English in style and is appropriately in Church Road, Earley, now part of Reading. The foundation stone was laid by the Hon Miss Mary Ann Ursula Addington, daughter of Viscount Sidmouth, on 20 April 1843 after a service conducted by the Vicar of Sonning, the Rev Hugh Nicholas Pearson. The Dean of Salisbury gave an address with a large crowd in attendance. The fabric used in the building is grey vitrified brick in the 76-feet-high north-west tower and the main body of the church, which was consecrated on 14 May 1844, although the aisles and chancel were added in 1882-83. The architect was John Turner.

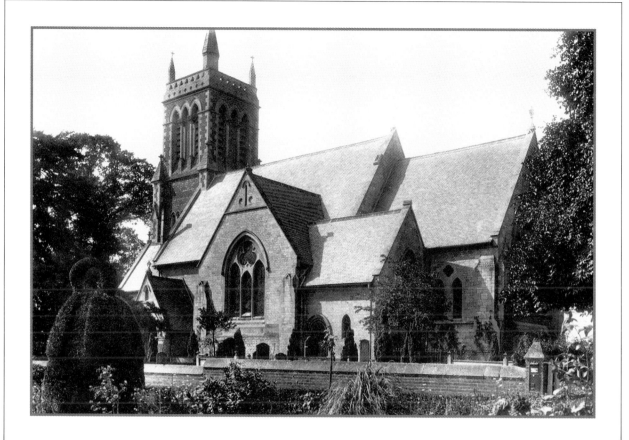

**EASTHAMSTEAD, THE CHURCH OF ST MICHAEL
AND ST MARY MAGDALENE 1901** 46901

Another imposing church inside and outside, St Michael and St
Mary Magdalene, Easthamstead, Bracknell, is a coarse Victorian
structure by J W Hugall, 1866-67. Parts of it are pre-Victorian,
including the west tower which is unusually high and a has an even
higher stair-turret halfway up. This brickwork gives it a Jacobean
flavour, but the tower is brick although the other parts of the
church are faced with ashlar.

◆

**EASTHAMSTEAD, THE CHURCH OF ST MICHAEL
AND ST MARY MAGDALENE 1901** 46902

Inside this expansive parish church the many signs of the Early
English era are manifest in the pulpit, for instance, which is
inscribed and dated 1631 on a large arched panel with a good
helping of arabesque. The stall backs are fine pedimented panels
dating from the 17th century, and came from Oxford Cathedral.
Stained glass in the east window represents the Last Judgement,
and is described as 'a noble but somewhat languid composition'.
Most of the figures are in white robes and the angels have wine-
coloured wings; the sky is dark blue. It is the work of Morris and
Co, which is Burne-Jones 1876, as is some of the other stained
glass. One example by Kempe of 1893 is said to be very feeble
compared to the Morris work.

ENGLEFIELD, ST MARK'S CHURCH C1955 E145001

A typical High Victorian estate church, St Mark's was built in 1857 by Sir George Gilbert Scott; he used a good deal of the 13th-century church which stood on this plot and which was probably surrounded by the old village. The design is Early English, and the interior is spacious and ornately furnished with interesting additions and memorials. The east windows have Purbeck marble shafts with rings and leaf capitals. Scott's church has a north tower with a stone broach spire and two tiers of lucarnes, making the building look stately and decidedly Victorian. Monuments include a knight with crossed legs in the south aisle, and Mrs Benyon in a scene depicting a lady collapsing on the ground and women attending her. There are many others which are worthy of note.

ETON,
THE COLLEGE CHAPEL 1895 35363

This magnificent building has a history all of its own. 'No part of Henry VI's scheme for a college was of greater importance than that of a church', according to the Eton Guide book. The charter was signed on 11 October 1440, and he laid the foundation stone on Passion Sunday 1441. Thomas Bekynton celebrated his first mass as Bishop of Bath and Wells on 13 October 1443. The King frequently changed his plans: the first building was pulled down when it was near completion for a new and larger one to be started. The choir of the new church was probably finished in about 1479, although it may have been in use earlier. Henry was overthrown in 1461, so building work probably stopped. The College was abolished by Papal Bull in 1463, but this decision was reversed in about 1470 after the college gained Royal favour from Edward IV. Provost Waynflete remained chief benefactor until his death in 1484, and he finished off the chapel. Lupton's Chapel was added in 1515, with its north and south-west porches; otherwise the main church remains much as Waynflete built it.

ETON,
THE COLLEGE CHAPEL 1906 56041

Despite having undergone several restorations over the years, including different floor levels and a general change along classical lines in 1699 by men closely connected with the Royal Office of Works, the interior has retained its grandeur. In 1905, the floor levels were restored at the east end and repaved with black and white marble in memory of those Etonians who fell in the South African war. In the mid-1800s, James Deacon restored the interior. He removed the paint and plaster from the roof, pulled down the classical organ loft and stripped the walls of the wooden panelling and seats to reveal the paintings. He erected new stained oak stalls with carved canopies, thirty-five per side. Stone flags were laid over the floor, and the whole choir was fitted with oak seats. On the east wall the Ten Commandments and the Beatitudes were painted, and a new organ was placed halfway up the south side of the choir. Time-bomb damage in 1940 required the replacement of the windows, except those in the northern side chapels, on the west over the organ and the south and south-west windows in the Ante-Chapel. In 1956 death watch beetle was discovered in the roof; the wood was replaced with light concrete vaulting concealing a steel-trussed and aluminium roof above.

ETON, THE COLLEGE CHAPEL, WALL PAINTINGS 1930 83433
Eton College Chapel's interior is as magnificent as its exterior. Low
wooden stalls along the walls of the choir accommodate the
College; a large expanse of bare wall was left to be filled with a
series of wall paintings. Pre-dating those in Winchester Cathedral,
the paintings are unique: grisaille, in part the work of William
Baker, they were done between 1479 and 1488. Later, the paintings
suffered from drastic treatment at the hands of the Reformers,
were wiped out in part in 1560, and were concealed by wainscoting;
they were re-discovered in the chapel restoration work of 1847. In
1923 the canopies of the stalls were taken down and what remained
of the paintings was completely uncovered and restored.

ETON, THE COLLEGE CHAPEL 1923 74816

A memorial window in the chapel contains some modern glass. In 1863, a gradual filling-in of the stained glass windows was begun. The north window, designed by Provost James, is based on the idea of a Cross of Light taken from Dante's 'Paradiso'. The glass is the work of H Grylls.

ETON, LOWER CHAPEL 1895 35343

As might be expected of the world's most famous English public school, Eton College chapels have a host of stories to tell about their early days. Lower Chapel, dedicated to St Mary the Virgin, was built in 1889-92. Queen Victoria and her daughters, Empress Frederick and Princess Beatrice, visited the new chapel on March 19, 1891, when the Empress unveiled a statue of the Queen over the gateway into the Quadrangle. Built of Sutton and Weldon stone from designs by Sir Arthur Blomfield, it is similar in some ways to the College chapel: Perpendicular in style, divided by large buttresses but without aisles. Three additional bays at the west end designed by Charles Blomfield were completed in 1926 to give seating for more than 500 boys. The roof is chestnut wood, and on the shields between the ribs are carved emblems of the Passion. At the west end there are dedications to a Head Master, Lower Master and assistant master dated around 1889. Much of the furniture and fixtures in the chapel were donated by Old Etonians and others connected with the school - organ, lectern, reredos, silver cross and candlesticks on the altar, frontal and superfrontal and processional cross. Brother, sisters and friends of Tom Cottingham Edwards-Moss put four stained glass windows in the chapel in 1895 'to preserve the memory of an Etonian so deeply mourned'. He died at the age of 31 after becoming MP for Widnes. The windows in the nave are by Kempe, and each depicts a virtue: on each are saints or men whose lives were examples of virtue, with scenes from the lives of these men. The detail is well worth further investigation. The tracery of the ten windows is perpendicular. That of the Chancel windows is decorated, given in memory of Mr Edwards-Moss, two representing the Annunciation and the shepherds of Bethlehem, one of whom is playing bagpipes. The sheaf in the window is the badge of Kempe. The tapestries - part of a memorial to those killed in the First World War - were designed by Lady Chilston and woven at the Morris works at Merton Abbey. The 'Eton Guide' describes the tapestries as a remarkable combination of the styles of the mid 16th century Brussels looms with English romantic detail, and quite untouched by developments in contemporary art; they form one of the latest examples of the power of the chivalric image in the 19th century public schools, showing the life of St George as typifying fallen Etonians.

ETON, ST JOHN'S CHURCH 1909 61408

In 1848, architect Benjamin Ferrey was commissioned to design a large church dedicated to St John the Evangelist on a site given by Eton College. The church had a nave and two aisles, a chancel and a tower with a tall spire. Total length, width and height were slightly larger than those of the College Chapel itself, and it could seat a larger number of people than the parish could supply. Original specifications were altered, money ran out and the interior of the church was almost bare for 10 years after the foundation stone was laid by the Prince Consort on October 21, 1852. Consecration took place two years later, with services taken by three of the college chaplains in turn week by week; there was no regular parson until 1875, when St John's was raised to the status of parish church. Strange to tell, 223 marriages had taken place since 1858, but they were not legally binding. So the Bishop of Oxford whisked a Bill through the House of Lords legalising the marriages before the public knew there was a problem.

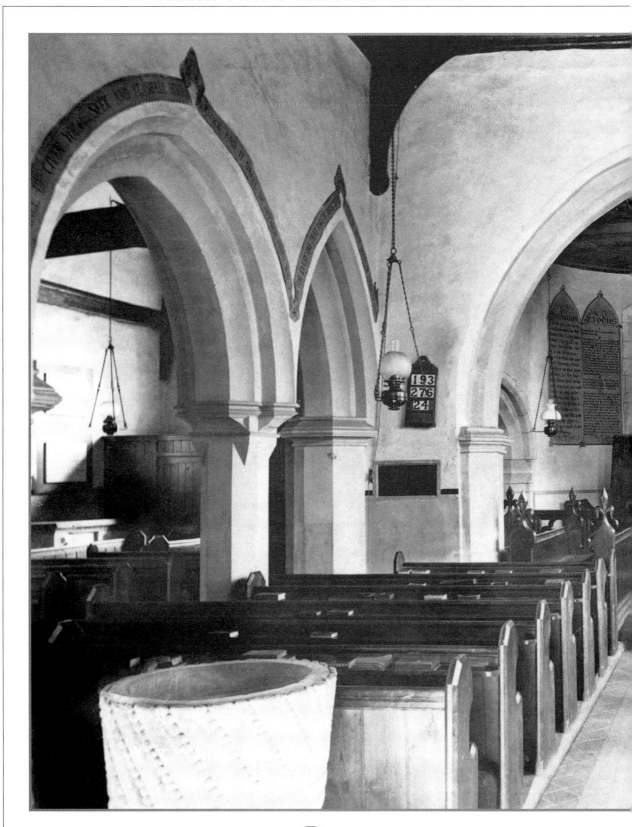

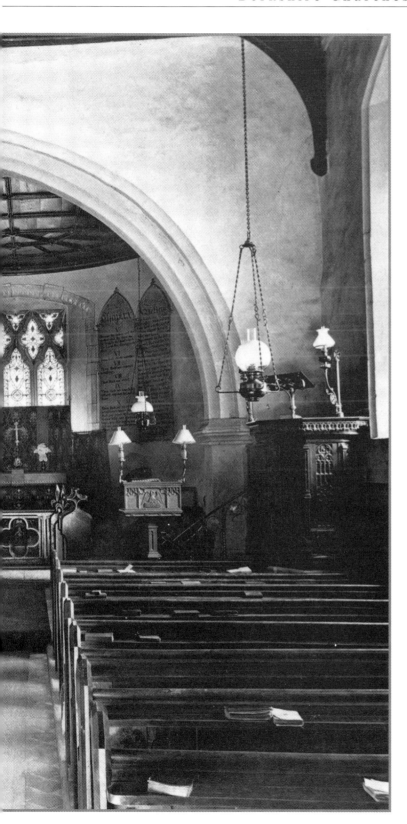

**FINCHAMPSTEAD,
ST JAMES 1910** 63007

This is a church with a Norman body and a brick tower built in 1720, with some overtones of the Perpendicular; the interior could well be of 1590 origin. The font is certainly Norman, tub-shaped and with beaded diagonal bands. One of the monuments is in memory of Elizabeth Blighe, 1635, and her little daughter. On the small brass plate Mrs Blighe is standing, holding the child by her hand and placing her other hand on a skull which lies on a column. A tomb chest with a black marble lid is dated 1670 and is the last resting place of Richard Palmer.

HAMPSTEAD NORRIS, THE VILLAGE FROM FOLLY HILL c1960 H149002

The village of Hampstead Norris nestles in a shallow valley, the buildings dominated by the short broad tower of St Mary's church in the background. For such a small village, St Mary's is quite a large church. It is overshadowed by its wide tower which has a flatly projecting staircase; it is of early construction, despite the Perpendicular doorway, window, and arch to the nave and battlements. Perhaps the south-west quoin of the nave is Saxon, and the south doorway is certainly reminiscent of the 1200s, as is the north doorway.

HAMPSTEAD NORRIS, ST MARY'S CHURCH c1950 H149004

The Early English chancel has lancets, which in the east wall are widely spaced in a trio with continuous roll mouldings inside. The nave roof is 1635 with collar beams, arched braces and pendants. St Mary's furnishings include an intriguing knight on horseback over 2ft high and from the 13th century. He is charging on a prancing horse, but his purpose remains a mystery. A faded painting depicts a large seated 13th-century figure of the Virgin against an arch.

HERMITAGE, HOLY TRINITY CHURCH C1955 H335021

HERMITAGE, HOLY TRINITY CHURCH C1955

This Norman-style church of about 1835 has long round-headed windows and a Norman west porch. The chancel, with brick dressings, is dated rather later at 1887, and is the work of Maurice Hulbert; it is claimed to be 'rather enterprising for the period'. The font is Neo-Norman.

HUNGERFORD, ST LAWRENCE'S CHURCH 1903

This photograph could well be a study in oils, but the church of St Lawrence, standing next to the canal, is said to be large and uninspired. It was designed and built by Pinch of Bath in 1816 and has a Bath stone exterior. Standing alone alongside the Kennet and Avon canal, this church is the main place of worship for the parish.

HUNGERFORD, ST LAWRENCE'S CHURCH 1903 49389

HUNGERFORD, ST LAWRENCE'S CHURCH C1955 H134006

Records show that St Lawrence stands on the site of a Christian church dating back to at least 1108. In 1325, Sir Robert de Hungerford repaired and refitted the south aisle as a chantry chapel, and another chantry was added in 1451. Many of the sepulchral monuments of the ancient church have been preserved and placed in the modern building, including the mutilated effigy and inscribed stone commemorating Sir Robert. The present church, designed by a Mr Pinch of Bath, replaced one demolished in 1814 and it was completed in 1816 in Bath stone. Disliked by Bishop Wilberforce, the church design has been improved upon.

MORTIMER COMMON, ST JOHN'S CHURCH C1955 M322009

This is an 1882 church by William Rhind. Only the aisle is left, because St John's had additions in 1896 by Swinfen Harris of a nave, chancel and west tower, in red brick. The tower had four top gables. Inside the church there is a painting by Nathaniel H J Westlake of Christ at Emmaus in the Nazarene tradition, showing a frontal of Christ with a cloth held by angels behind him. The stained glass is by Kempe.

NEWBURY, ST NICHOLAS'S CHURCH C1955 N61020

A monument of the wealth of Newbury in the late Middle Ages, St Nicholas is Perpendicular era throughout with large, ashlar-faced stonework, all work of 1500-32, and embattled throughout. The west tower has massive polygonal buttresses, and large pinnacles with their own battlements and smaller pinnacles. It carries the date 1532.

NEWBURY, ST NICHOLAS'S CHURCH C1955

The windows are four to six lights except in the clerestory, where they are grouped in three. The arcades have five bays and the piers are of a variety of standard-section four shafts and four hollows, in which the shafts towards the nave and aisle are trebled. Only one pier is different: it has a wave moulding instead of capitals only for the shafts. The chancel arch and the chancel roof are 1858 by Woodyer, but the nave roof is Perpendicular and has the initials J S for John Smallwood.

NEWBURY, ST NICHOLAS'S CHURCH C1955 N61032F

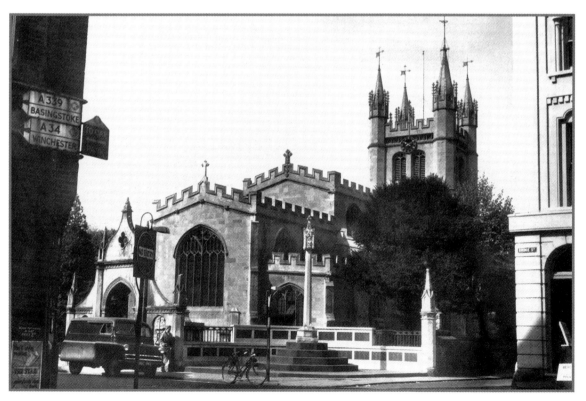

NEWBURY, ST NICHOLAS'S CHURCH 1956 N61077

NEWBURY, ST NICHOLAS'S CHURCH C1955 N61037F

From the street, the churchyard of St Lawrence is entered by two very pretty Gothic archways, probably connected with a payment to Fuller White in 1770,

NEWBURY, ST JOHN'S CHURCH C1965 N61088

Neither period nor modern, St John's church in Newtown Road is the inspiration of S E Dykes-Bower and dates from 1955-57, so it was fairly newly completed when this photograph was taken. The building is of red brick, largely reminiscent of neo-Romanesque, and does not have a great deal of charm, according to Nikolaus Pevsner.

OLD WINDSOR, ST ANDREW'S CHURCH C1965 O130059

The parish church of Clewer village, now part of Windsor, St Andrew's retains its village character in its old traditional setting. Built in flint, it is notable for its very short west tower and shingled broach spire. The ground floor has Norman windows reflecting the prominent Norman work inside, together with a north arcade of 1858 by Woodyer. Most of the exterior can be attributed to him, although the church is almost entirely mediaeval. In the churchyard, monuments include Quarter Master Edward Adams 1819, as a military still life, including an evidently lively horse. More recently, 1901 in fact, Canon T T Carter is recumbent in a miniature bronze relief including piers of the canopy detached in front of it; the work is attributed to W Bainbridge Reynolds.

PANGBOURNE, ST JAMES'S CHURCH 1890 27073A
Built in 1718, the tower of St James's is brick with brick quoins; it
has battlements with stone angles. The church itself is 1866, by
J Woodman; it is a spacious building, containing a Jacobean pulpit
with large blank arches and arabesque work.

PANGBOURNE, ST JAMES'S CHURCH 1910 62222

A monument of Sir John David, 1625, is large and in grey stone with three recumbent effigies, coupled Tuscan columns left and right, and a pediment. A remarkably reticent and classical tomb contains three daughters of Sir John Suckling; they died from 1658 to 1661. The black and white marble tablet has an open segmented pediment.

PANGBOURNE, ST JAMES'S CHURCH 1955 P5098

Near the church and catalogued as c1900 are Church Cottage and a group of houses and shops in a quiet, varied composition with grey headers and red brick. Stokes is the architect credited with their building.

PURLEY, ST MARY'S CHURCH C1955 P373004.

According to Nikolaus Pevsner in his book 'The Buildings of England - Berkshire', St Mary's is 'reached along a regrettable bungalowscape'. The imposing lychgate opens onto the spacious burial ground. Design and materials would be mostly 1870 by Street, and Pevsner claims it is not a church that could contribute to his fame.

PURLEY, ST MARY'S CHURCH C1955 P373006

Inside, the Norman chancel arch has single scallop capitals, strong roll moulding and an abacus with saltire crosses in chip carving, perhaps from the first half of the 12th century. The west tower is brick and dated 1626. One of the monuments is that of a family turning towards an urn on a high pedestal on which is the portrait of Anthony Storer, who died in 1818; a genius with an extinguished torch stands by the pedestal. There is no signature for this outstanding work.

READING, MARKET PLACE 1870 R13001

Reading is an ancient commercial centre for the cloth trade; it has a Cluniac abbey founded by Henry I in 1121, which became his favourite monastic establishment. An even older castle was destroyed in 1151. The town developed on the banks of the River Kennet away from the Thames water-meadows. The old Market Place is triangular and without visual distinction. At the centre is the Simeon Monument of 1804 designed by Soane, and to the left in the photograph is the Corn Exchange, which was built in 1854 following a debased Renaissance style.

**READING,
MARKET PLACE 1896** 37156
Between 1870 and 1896, the
photographs record more than subtle
changes, which include the
disappearance of Reed & Sons Hat
Warehouse and rebuilding to
accommodate the expansion of J S
Salmon & Son; but looking down the
Market Place, St Laurence's Church in
the background remains unchanged in
every detail.

READING, FRIAR STREET 1923 74440

This view from Friar Street puts St Laurence's Church into its full setting as part of the town centre. Originally, the outer abbey gate was attached to its south flank. The church was enlarged in 1196; this was probably connected with the establishment of the Hospitium of St John Baptist. The Perpendicular tower has polygonal buttresses and a tall arch to the nave, and a lower one to the north aisle embraces the tower. The arcade itself was rebuilt in 1522. The interior has additions throughout, although some have gone: an arcade of six arches known as Blagrave's Piazza along the west half of the south wall, built by Blagrave in 1619, was demolished in 1868.

READING, CHRIST CHURCH 1896 37163

An exceptionally rewarding High Victorian church and typical of Woodyer, Christ Church was built in 1861-62 and enlarged in 1874. It is large and imposing, with a north-west porch steeple of Early English style. The crockets of the gable over the porch entrance have remained uncarved.

READING, CHRIST CHURCH 1896 37164

Inside the church, arcade piers are closely set, built using Purbeck shafts and big capitals with many gablets and naturalistic flowers. A most astonishing and successful feature is the open-work tympanum in the chancel arch, an arched band of trefoils carrying some reticulation. Stained glass in the chancel and clerestory is by Hardman, 1868.

READING, THE CHURCH 1904 52009

**READING,
ST MARY'S BUTTS 1912** 64641

St Mary's has a south arcade dating
back to about 1200 and four bays with
round piers, capitals on the transition
from waterleaf to stiff-leaf, with
octagonal abaci and round arches with
one large chamfer. An arch of about
1300 must have connected a north
transept with an east chapel at the east
end of the north aisle. The chancel is
1864 and the north aisle 1872.
Although Norman, with a west tower as
late as 1550-53, the church is built of
chequered flint and stone with
polygonal buttresses. There are striking
monuments of William Kendrick with
two kneeling figures facing each other,
1635; the top pediment is segmental
and broken, but shows a transition
from Jacobean to Classical by its thick
garland. John Monk, 1809, is
commemorated by Flaxman with an
expiring man in a chair fortified by a
standing figure of Faith.

READING, THE CHILDREN'S POND, THAMES PROMENADE 1933 65924

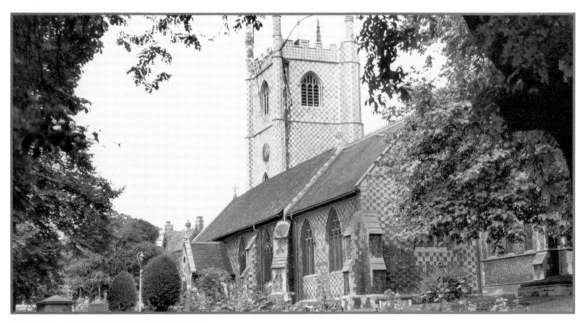

READING, ST MARY'S CHURCH C1955 R13056

This fine Episcopalian church in Castle Street is small with a sturdy tower. It dates back to 1798, but was mostly constructed in 1840-42, with original architecture by R Billing. The splendid Grecian facade has six giant Corinthian columns and a pediment, but the cupola has been lost. H and N Bryant are responsible for the portico and its surrounds.

RUSCOMBE, ST JAMES'S CHURCH C1960 R402028

Apart from the flint-built chancel, which is Norman, St James' nave and tower, which is in brick, were built in 1638-9. Yet the heavy wagon roof of the chancel is dated 14th century by the Victoria County History. It is fairly obvious that the two parts are not of the same build by the difference in the brickwork and by the way the west wall of the nave cuts through the buttresses of the tower. Inside, between the nave and the chancel the 17th-century tympanum carries the Ten Commandments. One remarkable monument is that of Sir James Eyre of 1799 by Sir Richard Westmacott. This noble piece has a large symmetrically-placed figure of a female standing by an urn and a branch of weeping willow.

SANDHURST, ST MICHAEL'S CHURCH 1906 57000

This church is built of coursed brown rubble and has a south-west tower with spire. Its interior has a lot of painting but is otherwise plain and uninspiring, according to Nikolaus Pevsner in his book on Berkshire buildings.

◆

SANDHURST, ST MICHAEL'S CHURCH 1939 88871

St Michael's dates back to 1853 and was designed by Street, but was later enlarged. An imitation Norman doorway in the porch entrance of the south-west tower may have been based on an original piece.

SANDHURST,
ST MICHAEL'S CHURCH C1955 S56016

Some people may not agree with Pevsner's description of the interior of St Michael's as being 'uninspiring'. The font is Norman and is said to have been 'executed by one of the daughters of the late Rector'. The painting on the walls is expansive, and the monuments include one memorial to Lady Farrer, 1892, in Athenian style. She is seated in a chair, with the family standing opposite. A Jacobean brass of 1608 is also worthy of note.

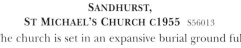

SANDHURST,
ST MICHAEL'S CHURCH C1955 S56013

The church is set in an expansive burial ground full of extravagant memorials.

SANDHURST, CHRIST CHURCH RMC CHAPEL 1901 46827

This amazing independent brick building is staggering by its sheer size, scale and style. The chapel is almost Byzantine in design, but its transepts are reminiscent of Italian Romanesque rather than Byzantine. In 1922, staff officer Captain A C Martin RE FRIBA conceived the extension; he completed the west end in 1937. Major General Sir Lionel Stopford, former Commandant before the war who returned to the college in 1917, suggested Captain Martin. Great efforts to raise funds were necessary during these lean years after the First World War. Inside, the sumptuous old apse has mosaics and marble revetments. The remainder is mostly white and a combination of alabaster and marble. Sir Hugh Casson's influence is evident: he designed the stands containing books of remembrance, and an imaginative and lively organ case, dating from 1950. This is the third chapel to be built at Sandhurst, and the second on this site; it has a history which in itself would fill a chapter and more. The present chapel stands as a living testimony to the devotion of many thousands of people from every corner of Britain and the former Commonwealth whose generosity built this inspiring place of worship.

◆

SLOUGH, ST MARY'S CHURCH C1965 s256053

St Mary's appears to have been constructed in three parts. W Stamp of Windsor started the building in 1835 as a brick neo-Norman structure; it was added to in 1876 when J O Scott started to replace it with a chancel and a two-bay nave on the east. The work was not completed until 1913, and included a new tower with a tall spire. Ay, there's the rub; for the church was paid for mainly by James Elliman of Elliman's Embrocation fame. Kempe was responsible for much of the stained glass which dates back to the 1880s. James Elliman's sister commissioned the stained glass in the west lancets: the four tall windows are filled with irregular abstract shapes in warm colours designed by Alfred Wolmark in 1915. Peacock-blue glass tiles surround the sanctuary, and the font is a grey onyx bowl with Irish green shafting and marble from Pavonazzo.

SLOUGH, GOSPEL TABERNACLE C1965 S256077

Of all the churches featuring in the Berkshire list, Slough's Gospel Tabernacle is the most modern, and therefore has the most recent history. Pastor W T Richards founded his church in 1943 in a Scout hut, and the present brick building in Pitts Road, now renamed as Slough Christian Centre, was built in 1964.

SONNING, ST ANDREW'S CHURCH 1890 27160

Sonning was a palace of the Bishops of Salisbury; excavations of the churchyard threw up evidence of a gatehouse of the late 15th century, a forecourt and great hall of an earlier date in the same century and a 13th-century range of chambers and kitchen.

SONNING, ST ANDREW'S CHURCH 1890 27162

St Andrew's is a very large church, visually Victorian and dating from 1853, designed by
Woodyer. It has some original Norman parts, such as the shaft of the pillar piscina with spiral
bands inside, and the bases of the north arcade piers; there is Early English work in the
lower part of the Perpendicular tower and the arch in the north of the chancel. A whole
architectural history would take in 13th-century aisle walling, early 14th-century south aisle
walls and late 14th-century parts in the north chapel, east chancel and aisle arcade piers on
both sides. Chancel decoration is by Bodley of around 1903-06. Screens in the north and
south chapels have been restored, but are Perpendicular with single light divisions. A brass
chandelier with two tiers is dated 1675, and the church has several splendid monuments, not
least the brass on the chancel floor of a figure of Laurence Fytton, 1434, and a set of Barkers
dated 1546, 1549 and 1580-something. A fragment of an Elizabethan monument shows six
small figures kneeling; Lady Litcott, 1630, in the south chapel is also shown kneeling below
curtains. Lady Anne Clarke, 1653, in the north chapel, is remembered with a bust in an oval
recess with garlands, over which is a segmental pediment. Charles and Elizabeth Rich, 1665
and 1656, in the north chapel, and Sir Thomas and Thomas Rich, 1667 and 1663, are under
the tower. A white recumbent effigy under an elaborate Gothic canopy linking chancel and
north chapel is dedicated to Canon Hugh Pearson, 1883.

STREATLEY,
ST MARY'S CHURCH 1890 27053
St Mary's has a short Perpendicular west tower, but much of the church is dated 1865 and was designed by Charles Buckeridge.

STREATLEY, ST MARY'S CHURCH 1896 38318

STREATLEY, ST MARY'S CHURCH 1896

The 1893 reredos is by Pearson, and the church has a remarkable painting of The Mourning of Christ after Van Dyck, the original of which hangs in the Berlin gallery. A brass of a 14in figure to Elizabeth Prout, 1440, is in the chancel north wall.

SUNNINGDALE, HOLY TRINITY CHURCH C1955

Coarse work of 1860 immediately strikes the visitor to Holy Trinity church. Designed by Street with competent additions in 1887-88 by J Oldrid Scott, it is a big church with a steeple over the crossing and much Early English detail.

SUNNINGDALE, HOLY TRINITY CHURCH C1955
S574011

SUNNINGDALE, HOLY TRINITY CHURCH C1955 S574037

The gates to the churchyard are cast iron and very obviously much older, perhaps from the previous church which was built on the site in 1839. Stained glass in one of the south windows is by Kempe, 1892.

SUNNINGDALE, HOLY TRINITY CHURCH C1960 S574041

Notable monuments include one of Prince Victor of Hohenlohe-Langenburg, 1891, in alabaster by his daughter Countess Feodora Gleichen. It is a recumbent figure in relief, and Italian Renaissance in style.

SUNNINGHILL, ST MICHAEL'S CHURCH 1901 46887

These three similar shots of St Michael's span half a century, but only in 1955 do we notice the restricted area of the burial ground around the church by the appearance of a substantial brick wall. St Michael's church is 1808 vintage, with additions of 1827-27. The yellow brick west tower has a re-used Norman zig-zag arch to the doorway.

SUNNINGHILL, ST MICHAEL'S CHURCH 1934 86326

The wide south aisle and the flat-topped, crenellated west front with Y window tracery is repeated in the north aisle. Some of the windows are Geometrical in style, and date from around 1888, when the chancel and south chapel were built in yellow brick with red brick trim. W H Crossland was the architect; he was responsible also for Royal Holloway College. From the imitation Perpendicular with complicated pinnacles to the interior thin cast iron columns, wide aisles, and original stucco roofs of 1828, to the nave roof of 1888 and the chancel roof, St Michael's church has had a busy life.

SUNNINGHILL, ST MICHAEL'S CHURCH 1955 A64029

In the churchyard, there are columns to Sir H R and Lady Popham; the latter died in 1866. The columns are carved in relief with nautical instruments and names of battles such as Copenhagen, Cape of Good Hope, North of Spain and Buenos Aires.

THATCHAM, ST MARY'S CHURCH C1955 T222011

This puzzling large, many-gabled flint-built church is the result largely of the restoration of 1857 by Thomas Hellyer. Original parts of the Norman south doorway with zig-zag moulding remain. The north arcade is also original, and clearly of the early 13th century. The first bay is low, and the others rather higher; the piers and arches have only a slight chamfer. There are signs of a former west wall east of the first bay.

THATCHAM, ST MARY'S CHURCH C1960 T222003

The Perpendicular north aisle has some windows, and in the south aisle on the west side there are stained glass windows by Powell of 1865. Tombstones include a chest with quatrefoils in the south chapel dedicated to the memory of Sir William Danvers, 1504, and Nicholas Fuller, 1620, has an alabaster tablet with kneeling figures of children below their parents.

THEALE, HOLY TRINITY CHURCH C1955 T254013

Ten years between these two photographs of Theale in the mid-20th century did little to change the appearance of Holy Trinity, which was designed by E W Garbett and built in 1820-32, with a tower by John Buckler added. It is another church remarkable for scale and style - and for its benefactor, Mrs Sophia Sheppard, who paid for it. She was the sister of Dr Routh, President of Magdalen College, Oxford and Rector of Theale.

THEALE, HOLY TRINITY CHURCH C1965 T254027

The pattern follows that of Salisbury Cathedral, although 1820 was better known for its Perpendicular. Holy Trinity is very tall; this is emphasised by its pairs of slender lancets in each bay and by the Salisbury-style buttresses. The tower is Early English in style, with an open passage on the ground floor and connected with the church by what seems to be a transept but is actually a library. The stone vaulted west porch dates the church with its high narrow proportions and handsome gallery inside.

TILEHURST, THE PARISH CHURCH OF ST MICHAEL c1955 T48009

St Michael's has a south aisle dating back to the early 14th century, its windows with Y and intersecting tracery, but the brick tower with clasping buttresses is 1737. The remainder of the building is 1856, designed by Street, including the rather wild spire with enlarged pinnacles, flying buttresses and very large lucarnes. Although not especially attractive either inside or out, the church has stained glass on the south and east in the chancel, and in the south aisle east window there is a Virgin and large angels on a patterned deep blue ground. The windows date from 1856. Sir Peter Valore, a merchant of Utrecht, has an alabaster monument of two recumbent effigies praying, with children below and in front left and right. The back arch has strap work and trophies.

TWYFORD, ST MARY'S CHURCH C1965

Built in flint in 1846 by Ferrey, St Mary's was enlarged considerably in 1908-10 by S S Stallwood. The style is Early English, and a north west tower dominates.

TWYFORD, ST MARY'S CHURCH C1965

The south aisle and arcade are by Ferrey. To the west of the church, which stands in a substantial surrounding burial ground, is a ruined tower said to belong to a former chapel of St Swithun.

TWYFORD, ST MARY'S CHURCH C1965   T331029

TWYFORD, ST MARY'S CHURCH C1965   T331092

WALTHAM, ST LAWRENCE'S CHURCH C1955 W377010

A majestic yew tree marks the approach to St Lawrence's, which has a west tower of flint and stone blocks topped with early brick. The doorway is definitively Perpendicular in style, but the west window is of 13th-century vintage with finely-detailed cusped intersecting tracery. The body of the church is flint with Victorian detail, including a bleak Victorian window of 1847 on the south transept front. Internally, the church shows its Norman origins with two-bay arcades north and south and unmoulded arches separated by pieces of wall. Two of the responds have a very elementary row of flat leaves. The arcades of the short Norman church were continued east by two standard Decorated bays, but no chancel arch. The font is Perpendicular, octagonal with no separate foot or stem and panelled sides. Of the pulpit, 1619, only the back panel with caryatids in its upper part is original. The tracery heads of the screen are original, and show their Decorated rather than Perpendicular origin. Abundant stained glass by Wailes, Kempe and M Schneider of Regensburg probably dates back to 1847 - a mysterious choice. Tombs and monuments include Sir Henry Neville, 1593, and two wives and a daughter, and Captain Henry Neville, 1809 - a military still life; Katherine Thomas, 1658, has a memorable monument with an urn of a curiously organic shape, somewhat like an inverted pear on a short marble column, placed in a niche with no ornament.

WARFIELD, ST MICHAEL'S CHURCH 1901 46909

Pevsner records St Michael's as one of the most rewarding churches around. It is constructed of dark brown conglomerate; the north aisle is Early English, established by the north lancet and traces of more lancets. The remainder is mostly Decorated, as can be seen in the north chapel and the chancel. One of the most ambitious designs of flowing tracery in Berkshire can be seen in the Y and cusped intersecting tracery in the chapel windows and the chancel. The Perpendicular west tower is of conglomerate and a lot of stone, and has a short recessed spire. Some of the church was over-restored by Street in 1872-75, but the effect is still generous in the continuous mouldings of typical breadth and details. Early 14th-century stained glass in the head of the east window is of angels, and some fragmentary 15th-century figures are discernible in the south transept window. Interesting monuments include Sir John B Walsh, 1825, by Bacon Jn., and Samuel Manning. This is a large tablet with the half-naked body of a male figure on a Greek couch, with Faith, perhaps, standing by. A John Walsh, who died in 1797, has a life-size female figure with an extinguished torch standing by an urn in front of an obelisk on his tomb.

◆

WARGRAVE, ST MARY'S CHURCH 1890 27179

The church of St Mary was burnt down in 1914 and rebuilt by W Fellowes Prynne. What remained of the old building was the brick west tower dating back to around 1635. It has polygonal buttresses and a re-set Norman north doorway with one order of colonnettes and zig-zag moulding, which had probably been moved. The scalloped capitals have shallow lobes and are hooded.

WARGRAVE, ST MARY'S CHURCH C1960 W25009

From the fire, a Norman north arcade was revealed which had plain slightly chamfered piers and plain arches. Hannen Mausoleum, designed by Lutyens, sits in the south east corner of the churchyard.

WARGRAVE, ST MARY'S CHURCH, INTERIOR c1960 W25018

A Perpendicular-style octagonal font with cusped quatrefoils, and mildly Expressionist stained glass in one south window by John Hayward, 1962, are among the finer interior fixtures of St Mary's. A dark church, its sombre timbered roof overshadows its timber furnishings.

WARGRAVE, THE VILLAGE 1890 27178

Timber-framed cottages and Georgian brick houses sit among striking contributions by Norman Shaw to Wargrave; they include Wargrave House, the former Vicarage and Woodclyffe Hall. Shaw's influence can be seen in Woodclyffe Hostel in Church Street, built in 1905 and designed by Cole A Adams.

WELLINGTON COLLEGE CHAPEL 1906 57021

An almost unknown architect, John Shaw, designed Wellington College; he intended to have the chapel projecting from the south range southwards at the east angle, and to match it by the infirmary projecting from the west angle. Wellington College was founded in 1853 as a national memorial to the Duke, who died in the previous year. The college is built of red brick and box stone and is in the style of Christopher Wren. The college's first headmaster, who became Archbishop of Canterbury, shied away from Shaw's concept and went to George Gilbert Scott in 1860. Scott was an enthusiast for the Gothic rather than the Classical style, but Prince Albert, who had wanted a reduced version of Eton Chapel and then of a basilica, agreed to the choice. The chapel was built in 1861-63 in red brick in the Geometrical style with a main apse and a north chapel apse and a very slender spire. The north chapel and apse were added in 1886 and 1899 by Arthur Blomfield. The interior has arcading and rising amphitheatre seating. The chapel is now part of a later group of school buildings to the east - dormitories, dining hall, common room and further additions of 1927 and 1940.

WINDSOR, ST GEORGE'S CHAPEL 1895 35384

As much could be written about St George's Chapel as would fill a book and still not be adequate; but as a start these rare early photographs show the full glory of this huge church. It was built to replace Henry III's chapel further east and was enlarged by Edward III; it had been needed when the Order of the Garter was created in 1348. The new chapel was begun in 1475 and built east to west, but slow progress meant that only a chancel without a vault had been completed by 1484. By 1503, the south transept was ready to receive the burial of Sir Reginald Bray, whose munificence made it possible to finish the nave. This gradual change is seen by the change of stone from the north transept to floor level. The chancel aisles must have been in use by then, because the bodies of John Schorne and Henry VI were transferred, and Edward IV's monument was in place.

WINDSOR, ST GEORGE'S CHAPEL 1895 35387

All seems to have been ready by 1511, despite the political vicissitudes of the times. In 1494, Henry VII decided to adapt the chapel of Henry II and Edward II as his tomb-house. Master mason Henry Janyns and the original designer William Vertue took on the work in 1478 and 1484. Restoration overshadows the details of the original carvers' work. Wren removed the original King's Beasts and repaired the roof and vaults after 1682; Emlyn repaired stonework and added a screen, stalls, and staircase to the Royal Pew from 1782-92. In 1841-45 Blore reconstructed the west window, and in 1863 Scott re-built the east end of the chancel. Then from 1866 to 1872 Scott put in a new west approach, and Pearson included new buttresses, parapets and gargoyles in 1878-86. The King's Beasts were completely restored from 1920-1930 by Brakspear.

WINDSOR CASTLE, ST GEORGE'S CHAPEL 1895 35393

The interior of St George's Chapel is wide rather than high, an effect partly due to the consistent use of four-centred arches. The stalls were provided in 1478-85, carved by William Berkely. They consist of three tiers, the topmost of which is for the Knights of the Garter and the dean and canons; the centre one is for the Military Knights, minor canons and the choirmen; and the lowest is for the choirboys. Behind the top row are high elaborate canopies with helmets and crests.

WINDSOR CASTLE, ST GEORGE'S CHAPEL 1895 35394

In front of the stalls are desks divided into blocks with a poppy head on each block end, with a scene to the west and another to the east, and small figures for prophets. The desk fronts have blank tracery with scenes in the tympana and spandrels carved in relief. All the stalls have misericords and carvings on the elbows of the seats; an inscription, mainly Psalm XX, runs along the front of the upper desks.

THE ALBERT MEMORIAL CHAPEL 1895 35411

Sumptuous in detail, with uniform repetitive arrangement, the monuments in St George's Chapel are awe-inspiring, to say the least. The Albert Memorial Chapel is rich in furnishings and decoration befitting such a room.

WINDSOR
THE ALBERT MEMORIAL CHAPEL 1895 35403

The Chapel abounds with monuments of beauty and dignity. They include the Princess Charlotte Memorial, 1817, by Matthew Cotes Wyatt, which combines the sensational with the chaste. This snow-white scene is acted by life-size figures. The Princess is lies dead on a ledge, covered entirely by a heavy sheet; only the fingers of one hand hang down from under it. Mourning women to left and right are completely hidden by mantles. Above, the Princess ascends to heaven, one breast bare; she is accompanied by two angels, one holding the stillborn baby, the other with crossed arms. The total effects are very strong, and the whiteness and lack of emotion on the faces are acceptable - as indeed is the scene created by the large and striking Prince Imperial's tomb pictured overleaf.

WINDSOR, THE ALBERT MEMORIAL CHAPEL 1895 35408

WINDSOR, ST JOHN BAPTIST, HIGH STREET 1895 35443

In 1820, Charles Hollis started building under the supervision of Wyatville. In 1869-73 the chancel was rebuilt and enlarged with a polygonal apse in the Decorated style by Teulon. St John Baptist's is built of brown stone, and has a west tower with oversized pinnacles. The windows are of many shapes and types. The interior contains much decoration, monuments, paintings, screens and railings; the unrecorded stained glass windows are early 20th-century.

WINDSOR, HOLY TRINITY CHURCH 1906 56033

Set in the middle of a wide square, Holy Trinity Church was built in 1842-44 by Blore, in the splendid isolation so much sought-after in the 19th century. It is described as a big clumsy yellow brick edifice with a west tower and spire. The wide interior has its galleries set between quatrefoil arcade piers carrying four-centred arches.

WINNERSH, ST CATHERINE'S CHURCH, BEAR WOOD C1955 W331026

Completed in 1846, St Catherine's Church was designed by J H Good Jnr. It cost £9,000 to build, paid for by Mr John Walter II, proprietor of The Times newspaper, whose daughter Catherine died at the age of 23 in 1844. The tower is nearly 90ft high, and the whole church is built in imitation mediaeval style. It was consecrated by Bishop Samuel Wilberforce, son of William, the famous and active abolitionist of the slave trade.

WINNERSH, ST CATHERINE'S CHURCH, BEAR WOOD C1955 W331028

A tablet in the church commemorates the founder, John Walter, who died in 1847 soon after the church was built. The stained glass windows in the nave are worthy of note. Another stained glass window in the tower is an abstract design by W Wailes. On the outside of the church are carved figures and heads just beneath the roof edge and gutter line. They include monsters and about 24 woodwooses, their heads draped in foliage. Other heads flank windows and doors.

WINNERSH, THE CHURCH OF ST MARY THE VIRGIN C1965 W330137

The church of St Mary the Virgin is comparatively new. The foundation stone was laid on 27 June 1965 by the Right Reverend Eric Knell, Lord Bishop of Reading. This photograph - one of the latest images in the Francis Frith Archive Collection - was taken in the same year. St Mary's was built as the result of great efforts by the Rev P W Trutwein and a Major Fowler.

WOKINGHAM, ALL SAINTS CHURCH 1906 57029

All Saints is Victorian in appearance outside. A dark brown conglomerate has been used for the west tower and the clerestory, suggesting that Woodyer's restoration of 1864-66 had some sympathy for the Norman period. It is suggested that a Norman doorway was provided using a few surviving stones.

WOKINGHAM, ALL SAINTS CHURCH C1955 W123015

Inside, the arcades are definitely mediaeval. The pier bases are Norman, and the round piers themselves may be 13th-century in their lower parts, but they were lengthened when the clerestory was built. Details of capitals and moulded arches suggest a 14th-century origin.

WOKINGHAM, ST PAUL'S CHURCH 1906 57030

Another Woodyer church, St Paul's is dated 1862-64 and is certainly a High Victorian building; it was given by John Walter of Bear Wood. Built of rock-faced stone, it has a north-east porch, a steeple and a spire bristling with pinnacled buttresses; the tower has 13th-century-style plate tracery.

WOKINGHAM, ST PAUL'S CHURCH C1955 W123095

The remainder is Decorative style, and not very attractive. Aisles were added in 1874; the arcades have quatrefoil piers with thin shafts in the diagonals and naturalistic leaf capitals, with ferns, geraniums and other work.

WOKINGHAM, ST SEBASTIAN'S CHURCH, NINE MILE RIDE 1910 62916

Nine Mile Ride runs east to west from south Easthampstead to south of the Arborfield Garrison, originally cutting through Windsor Forest; it is now developed with long lines of bungalows. Still, St Sebastian's church nestles along this route. From 1864 and by Butterfield, its nave and chancel are one. The building is of red and blue brick diapering, and it has a small bell turret with Jacobean balusters. The south porch is timber, and in the north aisle there are two wooden posts. The stained glass windows were designed by Gibbs.

WOOLHAMPTON, ST PETER'S CHURCH C1955 W376026

An unusual Berkshire church, Woolhampton's St Peter's has a bellcote with a spire on a stump made of flint.

WOOLHAMPTON, ST PETER'S CHURCH C1955 W376049

The church has many Early English-style details and a fancy timber porch; it dates from 1861, and was designed by John Johnson.

WOOLHAMPTON, ST PETER'S CHURCH C1965 W376068

WOOLHAMPTON, ST PETER'S CHURCH C1965

Inside the church, there is a chancel and two-bay arcade with low transepts. The font is part of a rebuilding process, but the stained glass in the west window is original 1861 by Willement.

WOOLHAMPTON, DOUAI ABBEY C1965

English Benedictines moved to Paris and then to Douai after the French Revolution; they returned to England in 1903, and took over the Catholic Diocesan College founded in 1838. The chapel dates from 1848, and is described as a humble building of nave and chancel. Inside, the altar is by Sebastian Pugin Powell, 1912-13, and there is a sculpture of the Virgin and Child as a demi-figure in stone in Italian Baroque style. The still, pictorial Crucifixion in the east window is of 1849; most of the glass in the Chapel looks French.

WOOLHAMPTON, DOUAI ABBEY C1965 W376072

WOOLHAMPTON, DOUAI ABBEY CHURCH C1965 W376077

The Abbey Church is by J Arnold Crush and was begun in 1928. The exterior is all brick, but the interior is white stone, which looks more conventional than the exterior. Building work is still in progress in this 1965 picture; a foundation stone was laid in 1964 for a lower nave and complete abbey buildings left and right of the church. The church was commissioned in 1963 and the design work was undertaken by Frederick Gibberd.

WRAYSBURY, ST ANDREW'S CHURCH C1955 W1500016

St Andrew's Church was almost wholly rebuilt in 1862 by Raphael Brandon. The stone spire is similar to the one he built at Datchet. Inside, the building is whitewashed and contains Victorian furnishings. By the chancel step is a brasswork of John Stonor dressed as a lawyer, not as an Eton scholar. Monuments include a dark pyramid with side urns of 1738, a delicate urn on a sarcophagus in a niche and the centre feature of an imposing composition by Kendrick in 1794, and an 1806 composition of a figure of Hope as a floridly-draped girl.

YATTENDON
ST FRIDESWIDE'S CHURCH, FRILSHAM C1960 Y32014

The site of this church on the edge of the sprawling tiny village of Frilsham dates
back to pre-Roman times, when sacrifices to Jupiter were offered. The circular
churchyard lends credence to this, as well as the rock outside the porch which may
have been the base of a special altar. The nave, chancel and sanctuary belong to the
Norman period, and the sanctuary was originally in the form of an apse. The windows
on the south wall of the nave are 15th-century. The church was restored in 1834 when
a brick tower and porch were added, and a mass dial can be seen on the left of the
south door. St Frideswide lived in Saxon Britain and died in 735. She founded an
abbey in Oxenford, now Oxford, and she is the patron saint of the city and its
university. Her commemoration date in the English church calendar is October 19,
and her shrine is in Christ Church Cathedral. She took refuge in a swineherd's hovel
in Frilsham woods after fleeing from her abbey with three nuns to escape the
attentions of a Pagan prince.

◆

Glossary of Terms

Abacus: flat slab.

Apse: vaulted semicircular or polygonal end of a chancel or chapel.

Arabesque: light and fanciful surface decoration, flowing lines, tendrils, etc, with vases and animals interspersed.

Arcade: range of arches supported on piers or columns, free standing.

Arch: round headed, semicircular; pointed; segmental; four-centred.

Ashlar: masonry of large blocks with even faces and square edges.

Atrium: inner court or open court in front of a church.

Aumbry: recess or cupboard to hold sacred vessels for Mass and Communion.

Ballflower: small globular flower of three petals enclosing small ball.

Basilica: an aisled church with a clerestory.

Belfry: turret on a roof to hang bells.

Bellcote: framework on a roof to hang bells from.

Block capital: Romanesque capital cut from a cube, lower angles rounded off to a circular shaft below.

Box pew: pew with high wooden enclosure.

Buttress: mass of brickwork or masonry projecting from or built against a wall for additional strength.

Cairn: mound of stones usually covering a burial.

Campanile: isolated bell tower.

Canopy: projection, hood over altar, pulpit, niche, statue, etc.

Capital: head or top of a column.

Cartouche: tablet with ornate frame usually enclosing an inscription.

Caryatid: whole female figure supporting an entablature.

Castellated: decorated with battlements.

Chamfer: surface made from cutting across the square angle of a stone or block of wood at an angle of 45 degrees.

Chancel: part of east end of church where altar is placed, applied usually to whole continuation of nave east of the crossing.

Chancel arch: at west end of chancel.

Chantry chapel: attached to, or inside a church for mass for the soul of the founder or other person.

Chevet: French for east end of church - chancel ambulatory, and radiating chapels.

Chevron: Norman moulding forming a zigzag.

Choir: that part of church where divine service is sung.

Cinquefoil: lobe formed by cusping of a circle or arch - the terms trefoil, quatrefoil, cinquefoil, express number of leaf shapes: 3, 4, 5.

Clerestory: upper storey of the nave walls of a church, pierced by windows.

Colonnade: range of columns.

Colonette: small column.

Cornice: in classical architecture the top section of the entablature. Also decorative feature along top of wall, arch, etc.

Crenellation: battlement.

Cross windows: one mullion and one transom.

Cupola: small polygonal or circular domed turret crowning a roof.

Entablature: in classical architecture, the whole of the horizontal members above a column - architrave, frieze or cornice.

Glossary of Terms

Fleche: slender wooden spire on centre of roof.

Fleuron: decorative carved flower or leaf.

Hood mould: projecting moulding above an arch or a lintel to throw off water.

Impost: bracket in a wall.

Keystone: massive stone in an arch or rib vault.

Lucarne: opening to let light in.

Lych gate: wooden gate structure with roof and open sides at entrance to churchyard providing space for receiving coffins.

Lynchett: long terraced strip of soil accumulating on downward side of prehistoric and medieval fields.

Misericord: bracket on underside of hinged choir stall seat - when turned up provides occupant with support during long standing. Also called miserere.

Nailhead: Early English ornamental motif of small pyramids repeated regularly.

Oriel: bay window.

Pediment: low-pitched gable.

Pier: strong solid support.

Pilaster: shallow pier attached to wall.

Pillar piscina: ornamental form crowning a spire, tower, buttress, usually steep pyramid, conical or similar.

Piscina: basin for washing Communion or Mass vessels, with drain, set in or against wall to south of altar.

Poppyhead: ornament of leaf and flower decorating tops of bench or stall ends.

Quoins: dressed stones at angles of buildings.

Reredos: structure behind and above altar.

Respond: half pier bonded into wall carrying one end of arch.

Roll moulding: semicircular or more than semicircular section.

Rose window: also wheel window. Circular tracery radiating from centre.

Saltire cross: equal limber cross diagonally placed.

Scagliola: plaster or cement and colouring to resemble or imitate marble.

Screen: separation between chapel and remainder of church.

Sedilia: seats for priest on south side of chancel.

Spandrel: triangular surface between side of arch, horizontal drawn from apex and vertical drawn from its springer. Also surface between two arches.

Stiff leaf: Early English type of foliage of many-lobed shapes.

Strapwork: 16th century decoration of interlaced bands, forms similar to fretwork or cut and bent leather.

Tomb chest: stone coffin.

Tourelle: turret corbelled out of wall.

Tracery: intersecting ribwork in upper part of window or decorative work in blank arches, vaults.

Tympanum: space between lintel and arch above doorway.

Wainscot: timber lining to walls.

Waterleaf: leaf shape in later 12th-century capitals, broad, unribbed, tapering; curving up towards the angle of the abacus and turned in at top.

Index

Frith Book Co Titles

Frith Book Company publish over a 100 new titles each year. For latest catalogue please contact Frith Book Co.

Town Books 96pp, 100 photos. County and Themed Books 128pp, 150 photos (unless specified) All titles hardback laminated case and jacket except those indicated pb (paperback)

Around Barnstaple	1-85937-084-5	£12.99
Around Blackpool	1-85937-049-7	£12.99
Around Bognor Regis	1-85937-055-1	£12.99
Around Bristol	1-85937-050-0	£12.99
Around Cambridge	1-85937-092-6	£12.99
Cheshire	1-85937-045-4	£14.99
Around Chester	1-85937-090-X	£12.99
Around Chesterfield	1-85937-071-3	£12.99
Around Chichester	1-85937-089-6	£12.99
Cornwall	1-85937-054-3	£14.99
Cotswolds	1-85937-099-3	£14.99
Around Derby	1-85937-046-2	£12.99
Devon	1-85937-052-7	£14.99
Dorset	1-85937-075-6	£14.99
Dorset Coast	1-85937-062-4	£14.99
Around Dublin	1-85937-058-6	£12.99
East Anglia	1-85937-059-4	£14.99
Around Eastbourne	1-85937-061-6	£12.99
English Castles	1-85937-078-0	£14.99
Around Falmouth	1-85937-066-7	£12.99
Hampshire	1-85937-064-0	£14.99
Isle of Man	1-85937-065-9	£14.99
Around Maidstone	1-85937-056-X	£12.99
North Yorkshire	1-85937-048-9	£14.99
Around Nottingham	1-85937-060-8	£12.99
Around Penzance	1-85937-069-1	£12.99
Around Reading	1-85937-087-X	£12.99
Around St Ives	1-85937-068-3	£12.99
Around Salisbury	1-85937-091-8	£12.99
Around Scarborough	1-85937-104-3	£12.99
Scottish Castles	1-85937-077-2	£14.99
Around Sevenoaks and Tonbridge	1-85937-057-8	£12.99

Sheffield and S Yorkshire	1-85937-070-5	£14.99
Shropshire	1-85937-083-7	£14.99
Staffordshire	1-85937-047-0 (96pp)	£12.99
Suffolk	1-85937-074-8	£14.99
Surrey	1-85937-081-0	£14.99
Around Torbay	1-85937-063-2	£12.99
Wiltshire	1-85937-053-5	£14.99
Around Bakewell	1-85937-113-2	£12.99
Around Bournemouth	1-85937-067-5	£12.99
Cambridgeshire	1-85937-086-1	£14.99
Essex	1-85937-082-9	£14.99
Around Great Yarmouth	1-85937-085-3	£12.99
Hertfordshire	1-85937-079-9	£14.99
Isle of Wight	1-85937-114-0	£14.99
Around Lincoln	1-85937-111-6	£12.99
Oxfordshire	1-85937-076-4	£14.99
Around Shrewsbury	1-85937-110-8	£12.99
South Devon Coast	1-85937-107-8	£14.99
Around Stratford upon Avon	1-85937-098-5	£12.99
West Midlands	1-85937-109-4	£14.99

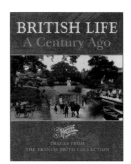

British Life A Century Ago
246 x 189mm
144pp, hardback.
Black and white
Lavishly illustrated with photos from the turn of the century, and with extensive commentary. It offers a unique insight into the social history and heritage of bygone Britain.

1-85937-103-5 £17.99

Available from your local bookshop or from the publisher

Frith Book Co Titles Available in 2000

Around Bath	1-85937-097-7	£12.99	Mar
Cumbria	1-85937-101-9	£14.99	Mar
Down the Thames	1-85937-121-3	£14.99	Mar
Around Exeter	1-85937-126-4	£12.99	Mar
Greater Manchester	1-85937-108-6	£14.99	Mar
Around Harrogate	1-85937-112-4	£12.99	Mar
Around Leicester	1-85937-073-x	£12.99	Mar
Around Liverpool	1-85937-051-9	£12.99	Mar
Northumberland and Tyne & Wear			
	1-85937-072-1	£14.99	Mar
Around Oxford	1-85937-096-9	£12.99	Mar
Around Plymouth	1-85937-119-1	£12.99	Mar
Around Southport	1-85937-106-x	£12.99	Mar
Welsh Castles	1-85937-120-5	£14.99	Mar
Canals and Waterways	1-85937-129-9	£17.99	Apr
Around Guildford	1-85937-117-5	£12.99	Apr
Around Horsham	1-85937-127-2	£12.99	Apr
Around Ipswich	1-85937-133-7	£12.99	Apr
Ireland (pb)	1-85937-181-7	£9.99	Apr
London (pb)	1-85937-183-3	£9.99	Apr
New Forest	1-85937-128-0	£14.99	Apr
Around Newark	1-85937-105-1	£12.99	Apr
Around Newquay	1-85937-140-x	£12.99	Apr
Scotland (pb)	1-85937-182-5	£9.99	Apr
Around Southampton	1-85937-088-8	£12.99	Apr
Sussex (pb)	1-85937-184-1	£9.99	Apr
Around Winchester	1-85937-139-6	£12.99	Apr
Around Belfast	1-85937-094-2	£12.99	May
Colchester (pb)	1-85937-188-4	£8.99	May
Exmoor	1-85937-132-9	£14.99	May
Leicestershire (pb)	1-85937-185-x	£9.99	May
Lincolnshire	1-85937-135-3	£14.99	May
North Devon Coast	1-85937-146-9	£14.99	May
Nottinghamshire (pb)	1-85937-187-6	£9.99	May
Peak District	1-85937-100-0	£14.99	May
Around Truro	1-85937-147-7	£12.99	May
Yorkshire (pb)	1-85937-186-8	£9.99	May

Berkshire (pb)	1-85937-191-4	£9.99	Jun
Brighton (pb)	1-85937-192-2	£8.99	Jun
County Durham	1-85937-123-x	£14.99	Jun
Dartmoor	1-85937-145-0	£14.99	Jun
Down the Severn	1-85937-118-3	£14.99	Jun
East London	1-85937-080-2	£14.99	Jun
East Sussex	1-85937-130-2	£14.99	Jun
Glasgow (pb)	1-85937-190-6	£8.99	Jun
Kent (pb)	1-85937-189-2	£9.99	Jun
Kent Living Memories	1-85937-125-6	£14.99	Jun
Redhill to Reigate	1-85937-137-x	£12.99	Jun
Stone Circles & Ancient Monuments			
	1-85937-143-4	£17.99	Jun
Victorian & Edwardian Kent			
	1-85937-149-3	£14.99	Jun
Victorian & Edwardian Maritime Album			
	1-85937-144-2	£17.99	Jun
Victorian & Edwardian Yorkshire			
	1-85937-154-x	£14.99	Jun
West Sussex	1-85937-148-5	£14.99	Jun
Churches of Berkshire	1-85937-170-1	£17.99	Jul
Churches of Dorset	1-85937-172-8	£17.99	Jul
Derbyshire (pb)	1-85937-196-5	£9.99	Jul
Edinburgh (pb)	1-85937-193-0	£8.99	Jul
Folkstone	1-85937-124-8	£12.99	Jul
Gloucestershire	1-85937-102-7	£14.99	Jul
Herefordshire	1-85937-174-4	£14.99	Jul
North London	1-85937-206-6	£14.99	Jul
Norwich (pb)	1-85937-194-9	£8.99	Jul
Ports and Harbours	1-85937-208-2	£17.99	Jul
Somerset and Avon	1-85937-153-1	£14.99	Jul
South Devon Living Memories			
	1-85937-168-x	£14.99	Jul
Warwickshire (pb)	1-85937-203-1	£9.99	Jul
Worcestershire	1-85937-152-3	£14.99	Jul
Yorkshire Living Memories			
	1-85937-166-3	£14.99	Jul

FRITH PRODUCTS & SERVICES

Francis Frith would doubtless be pleased to know that the pioneering publishing venture he started in 1860 still continues today. More than a hundred and thirty years later, The Francis Frith Collection continues in the same innovative tradition and is now one of the foremost publishers of vintage photographs in thc world. Some of the current activities include:

Interior Decoration

Today Frith's photographs can be seen framed and as giant wall murals in thousands of pubs, restaurants, hotels, banks, retail stores and other public buildings throughout the country. In every case they enhance the unique local atmosphere of the places they depict and provide reminders of gentler days in an increasingly busy and frenetic world.

Product Promotions

Frith products have been used by many major companies to promote the sales of their own products or to reinforce their own history and heritage. Brands include Hovis bread, Courage beers, Scots Porage Oats, Colman's mustard, Cadbury's foods, Mellow Birds coffee, Dunhill pipe tobacco, Guinness, and Bulmer's Cider.

Genealogy and Family History

As the interest in family history and roots grows world-wide, more and more people are turning to Frith's photographs of Great Britain for images of the towns, villages and streets where their ancestors lived; and, of course, photographs of the churches and chapels where their ancestors were christened, married and buried are an essential part of every genealogy tree and family album.

A series of easy-to-use CD Roms is planned for publication, and an increasing number of Frith photographs will be able to be viewed on specialist genealogy sites. A growing range of Frith books will be available on CD.

Frith Products

All Frith photographs are available Framed or just as Mounted Prints, and can be ordered from the address below. From time to time other products - Address Books, Calendars, Table Mats, etc - are available.

The Internet

Already thousands of Frith photographs can be viewed and purchased on the internet. By the end of the year 2000 some 60,000 Frith photographs will be available on the internet. The number of sites is constantly expanding, each focussing on different products and services from the Collection.

Some of the sites are listed below.

www.townpages.co.uk
www.icollector.com
www.barclaysquare.co.uk
www.cornwall-online.co.uk

For more detailed information on Frith companies and products, look at these sites:

www.francisfrith.co.uk
www.frithbook.co.uk
www.francisfrith.com

See the complete list of Frith Books at:

www.frithbook.co.uk

This web site is regularly updated with the latest list of publications from the Frith Book Company Ltd. If you wish to buy books relating to another part of the country that your local bookshop does not stock, you may purchase on-line.

For further information, trade, or author enquiries please contact us at the address below:
The Francis Frith Collection, Frith's Barn, Teffont, Salisbury, Wiltshire, England SP3 5QP.
Tel: +44 (0)1722 716 376 Fax: +44 (0)1722 716 881 Email: uksales@francisfrith.com

To receive your FREE Mounted Print

Mounted Print
Overall size 14 x 11 inches

Cut out this Voucher and return it with your remittance for £1.50 to cover postage and handling. Choose any photograph included in this book. Your SEPIA print will be A4 in size, and mounted in a cream mount with burgundy rule lines, overall size 14 x 11 inches.

Order additional Mounted Prints at HALF PRICE (only £7.49 each*)

If there are further pictures you would like to order, possibly as gifts for friends and family, acquire them at half price (no additional postage and handling required).

Have your Mounted Prints framed*

For an additional £14.95 per print you can have your chosen Mounted Print framed in an elegant polished wood and gilt moulding, overall size 16 x 13 inches (no additional postage and handling required).

---

* IMPORTANT!
These special prices are only available if ordered using the original voucher on this page (no copies permitted) and at the same time as your free Mounted Print, for delivery to the same address

---

Frith Collectors' Guild

From time to time we publish a magazine of news and stories about Frith photographs and further special offers of Frith products. If you would like 12 months FREE membership, please return this form.

Send completed forms to:
The Francis Frith Collection, Frith's Barn, Teffont, Salisbury, Wiltshire SP3 5QP

Voucher for FREE and Reduced Price Frith Prints

Picture no.	Page number	Qty	Mounted @ £7.49	Framed + £14.95	Total Cost
		1	**Free of charge***	£	£
			£7.49	£	£
			£7.49	£	£
			£7.49	£	£
			£7.49	£	£
			£7.49	£	£

	* Post & handling	£1.50
Book Title	**Total Order Cost**	£

Please do not photocopy this voucher. Only the original is valid, so please cut it out and return it to us.

I enclose a cheque / postal order for £ . . . .
made payable to 'The Francis Frith Collection'
OR please debit my Mastercard / Visa / Switch / Amex card

Number . . . .

Expires . . . . Signature . . . .

Name Mr/Mrs/Ms . . . .

Address . . . .

. . . .

. . . .

. . . .

. . . . Postcode . . . .

Daytime Tel No . . . .   Valid to 31/12/01

The Francis Frith Collectors' Guild

Please enrol me as a member for 12 months free of charge.

Name Mr/Mrs/Ms . . . .

Address . . . .

. . . .

. . . .

. . . . Postcode . . . .

Free Print - see overleaf